HORSE-MAD GI

Everything You Need to kno

By Olivia Gra

CW00865678

Copyright

© Copyright 2018 - All rights reserved.

The contents of this book may not be reproduced, duplicated or transmitted without direct written permission from the author. Under no circumstances will any legal responsibility or blame be held against the publisher for any reparation, damages, or monetary loss due to the information herein, either directly or indirectly.

Legal Notice:
This book is copyright protected. This is only for personal use. You cannot amend, distribute, sell, use, quote or paraphrase any part or the content within this book without the consent of the author.

Disclaimer Notice:
Please note the information contained within this document is for educational and entertainment purposes only. Every attempt has been made to provide accurate, up to date and reliable complete information. No warranties of any kind are expressed or implied. Readers acknowledge that the author is not engaging in the rendering of legal, financial, medical or professional advice. The content of this book has been

derived from various sources. Please consult a licensed professional before attempting any techniques outlined in this book.

By reading this document, the reader agrees that under no circumstances is the author responsible for any losses, direct or indirect, which are incurred because of the use of information contained within this document, including, but not limited to, —errors, omissions, or inaccuracies.

Table of Contents

Introduction

Hi Girls

Welcome to the Horse Mad Girls Club!

I figured that there would be no one better person than my eight-year-old daughter to introduce this fantastic book to you.

She is completely mad about horses. She is so mad about horses that she drives me mad! Her bedroom is covered with photos of different kinds of horses, she goes riding every week, and she is crazy about *Schleich* models and all things horsey! They are all over the house! I bet she is just like you!

Together we put this book together for YOU, so that you can have all the information that you need, to be knowledgeable about horses. There are even places in it for you to make notes! Now that you have this book, if anyone asks you a question about horses, you can be the first to answer.

We also put "The Horse Mad Girls Club" together so that you can find out what you could be when you are a grown up, if you still love horses. There are so many different options available for horse lovers!

So, without any further delay... over to you Gracie!

Letter from Gracie

Hi Girls Club

My name is Gracie and I am thrilled to be a part of this book!

Horses are beautiful animals and I can't understand why anybody wouldn't like them. I started liking horses when I was 5. I was looking at some pictures and just thought that they were amazing. From that time on my love for horses has grown. If you walked into my room you would know straight away that they are my first love.

I love this book because it not only tells me interesting facts about horses, but I can also write my own notes and it gives me practical advice on how to look after horses.

I have been able to include wonderful facts on my favourite horses that you will read of in the 'Breed under the microscope' section.

When I grow up I would love to be a championship horse rider and I would love to help animals if they are sick, hurt or wondering out in the streets. In the book you can find loads of jobs that you could do when you are older that involve the care of horses.

Welcome to the MAD HORSE GIRL CLUB!
I hope you enjoy it

Gracie!

Quiz

This quiz helps you to work out whether or not you are really, really Horse Mad. There are some people that just like horses. There are some people that just put up with horses. There are some people that just pretend to like horses because everyone else does. We need to make sure that you are really HORSE MAD! To help us do this please answer the questions below.

Go through it with a friend if you need to!

1. What do you dream of when you go to sleep?
   a) Cuddly Toys

b) Chocolate

(c) Horses)

2. What do you really want for Christmas?

   a) iPad

   b) Hover Board

   (c) Horse)

3. What is your bedroom wall covered with?

   (a) Your favourite Pop Star)

   b) Pictures of Horses

   c) Nothing

4. What programs do you always look for when you go on Netflix?

   a) Cartoons

   (b) Horse Films)

   c) Disney

5. What programs do you always look for when you go on YouTube?

   (a) How to draw Horses)

   b) Computer games

   c) Music Videos

6. When you are in the car staring out the window, what would cause you to scream out and make everyone aware if you saw one?

a) A horse

b) A dog

c) A cat

7. When you have time to draw whatever you want, what do you draw?

a) Cartoon Pictures

b) Horses

c) Princesses

8. What animal was in the last two books you read?

   a) Horse

   b) Dog

   c) Frog

9. You sleep with a fluffy toy which is a...?

   a) Bear

   b) Horse/Unicorn

   c) Dinosaur

10. What animal is on your favourite T-shirt?

   a) Deer

   b) Horse/Unicorn

   c) Dog

If most of your answers are the word Horse or Unicorn then I have the honour of telling you that quite positively, quite absolutely, you are HORSE MAD!

Welcome to the sisterhood!

Let's get started!

A Horsey Introduction

Some people believe that horses evolved and are product of a revolutionary change stretching back for thousands of years. Some people believe that they were just simply made by God. What I know is that they are the most beautiful creation of all. Apart from us of course!

The evolution of the horse is fascinating and many brainy people all over the world are still captivated by it. In North America wonderful fossil deposits can be found of horses that died many centuries ago. In addition to this, in London in 1839 there was a discovery made by Sir Richard Owen, a palaeontologist, who found another wonderful amount of bones from what is believed to be the earliest horses of all.

What we do know for a fact is that horses have come a long way from when they were first put on this earth. They have been through many things and fulfilled many roles helping mankind develop through the centuries.

Some believe there is a special connection between human beings and horses, just as there is with Dogs and humans, this could be one of the reasons why you are horse mad .

Horses are as varied as humans. Just as we have big humans and small humans, we have big horses and small horses. Just as we have different colours of people, we have different colours of horses. Just as we have different races of people, so we have different breeds of horses across different world regions. This could be why horses appeal to many girls and boys across the world, because it is easy find horse to fall in love with!

How to draw a Horse

As a horse lover I am sure you love to draw horses ALL the time. This is how to draw a **Horse** in 8 easy steps.

This is a simple way to start drawing horses of all different kinds. Remember, take your time. Practice makes perfect.

Step 1: Start by drawing the head of the Horse.

1

Step 2: Draw the neck.

Step 3: Draw the upper neck and lower back towards the tail.

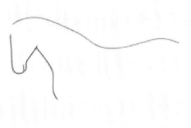

Step 4: Draw the beginning of the front legs and the back legs.

Step 5: Add some lines to the front and back legs and don't forget to add the ear.

Step 6: Finish the belly and the 2 legs and hooves.

Step 7: Draw the 2nd set of legs.

Step 8: End by drawing the mane and tail to complete this drawing of the Horse.

Keep practicing, because once you get good it will be time for you to draw your DREAM HORSE!

What is your Dream horse?

I am sure that you have had loads of dreams about your dream horse. Maybe you were riding through the countryside, or riding along the beach, your hair blowing in the wind. Maybe in your dream your horse could talk or even fly!

Here is an opportunity for you to describe your dream horse.

What does it look like?

What is its name?

What colour is it?

Does it have a personality?

What does it eat?

Can it talk?

What makes it special to you?

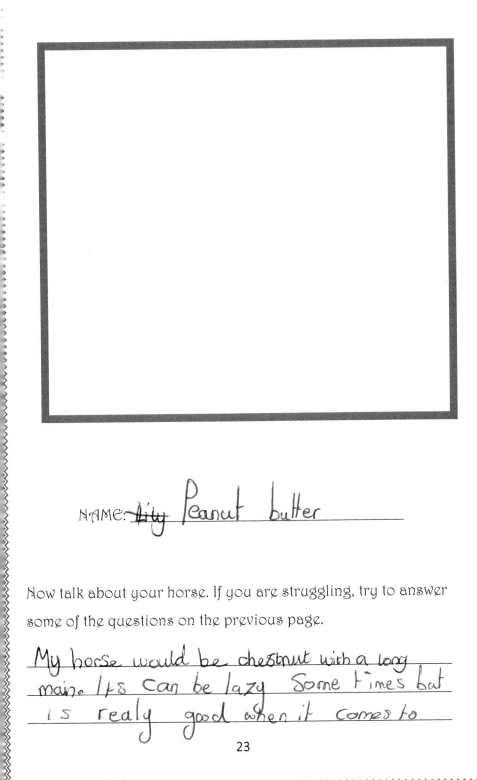

NAME: ~~Lily~~ Peanut butter

Now talk about your horse. If you are struggling, try to answer some of the questions on the previous page.

My horse would be chestnut with a long main. Its can be lazy Some times but is realy good when it comes to

23

Jumping. His nick name is peanut and is so good with people. He lores it when you wear watermelon pink or sky blue. His Enemy is this horse called Ginger and she only lives 3 stables away as peanut butters best friend is a horse called Queen and lives in one of the feilds.

Words for Horse in Different Languages

Many girls across the world love horses, not just ones where you live. Below we have put together a list of how people across the world say "Horse" in different languages. Why not see if you can pronounce them correctly!

Language	Ways to say horse	Language	Way to Say Horse
Basque	zaldi	Albanian	kalë
Bosnian	konj	Bulgarian	кон
Catalan	cavall	Croatian	konj

27

Czech	kůň	Danish	hest
Dutch	paard	Estonian	hobune
Finnish	hevonen	French	cheval
Galician	caballo	German	Pferd
Greek	άλογο(álogo)	Hungarian	ló
Icelandic	Hestur	Irish	capall
Italian	cavallo	Latvian	zirgs
Lithuanian	arklys	Macedonian	коњ
Maltese	żiemel	Norwegian	hest
Polish	koń	Portuguese	cavalo
Romanian	cal	Russian	лошадь(loshad')
Serbian	коњ(konj)	Slovak	kôň
Slovenian	konj	Spanish	caballo
Swedish	häst	Ukrainian	кінь(kin')
Welsh	ceffyl	Yiddish	פערד
Afrikaans	perd	Chichewa	kavalo
Hausa	doki	Igbo	inyinya
Sesotho	pere	Somali	faras
Swahili	farasi	Yoruba	ẹṣin
Zulu	ihhashi	Maori	hoiho
Filipino	kabayo	Indonesian	kuda
Javanese	jaran	Malagasy	soavaly
Malay	kuda		

Breed Under the Microscope

BREED: FRIESIAN

Warmblood

Origin: The Netherlands

Height: Approximately 15HH

Colour: Black

Physique: Round Hind, Good bone Structure, Long flowing head, Full Mane and tail, Crested neck

Temperament: Hard working, great temperament

Jobs: All-round horse work, circus, riding, driving.

The Friesian is the grandad of horses. It is now one of the oldest horses in Europe. Used as a warhorse, Roman historians found evidence of this beautiful horse being used at Hadrian's wall in Great Britain around 150 CE. Its nickname is the 'Blackpearl of the Netherlands'.

5 Facts About Horses

Horses can sleep both lying down and standing up!

Horses have around 205 bones in their skeleton

Domestic Horses have a lifespan of around 25 years

The fastest recorded sprinting speed of a horse was 55mph

It is estimated that there are over 60 million horses in the world

Best Horses Names

Horses have the best names. In some cases, they have 2 names. One name for competition and their real name. What is your favourite horse name?

When naming a horse, you want to choose a name that will fit them perfectly. Maybe it will be one that suits their character, breed or personality. Here are some fantastic horse names broken down by types. Which ones do you like? Write down your favourite 3 at the end of the list!

Brown Horse Names

- CHOCOLATE
- FUDGE
- MISTY
- COCOA
- BROWNIE
- HAZEL
- CLEVELAND
- ADOBE
- CINNAMON
- KIT KAT
- BRANDY

Black Horse Names

BLACKY   BEAUTY

MIDNIGHT   JAGUAR

NOIR   EBONY

Chestnut Horse Names

- CHESTNUT
- AUTUMN
- JANE
- FIONA
- LYNDA
- RUSSELL

Buckskin Horse Names

- DAMZEL
- BLONDIE
- RAPUNZEL
- CANDY

- SPIRIT
- LIGHTHEART
- DEBBIE

Grey Horse Names

- TREVOR
- STORM CLOUD
- PEPPER
- SNOWBALL
- LACEY
- BONNEY
- JOJO

Horse Type Name

Many horsey people like to name their horses something that relates to their breed. Some breeds have a specific 'style' of name; for example, Welsh Ponies often have Welsh-inspired names and spellings. Here are a few for you to look at!

Racing Horse Names

- BOLT
- CHALLENGER
- SPEED
- USAIN
- FARGO

- JET
- VICTORY

Western Frontier Horse Names

- GOLDY
- LEX
- CHAMP
- OAKLEY
- RIO
- DALE
- GENE
- CASH

PERSONALITY NAMES

Just like many people are named after their personally, it's the same with horses. These lists are just the beginning why not use them as inspiration!

Posh Horse Names

- ELIZABETH
- CHALSTON
- BRUCE
- CHARLES
- RANDOLPH
- PRINCE

- HARRY
- MARQUIS
- PHILIP
- KINGSLEY

Funny Horse Names

- CHICKA LYNDA
- BOMERANG
- MOMO
- BOBO
- BARNABY
- NEWTON
- TIGGER
- BUSTER
-

Names for Well-Travelled Horses

- PARIS
- SICILY

- BEIJING
- VANCOUVER
- UTAH
- SYDNEY
- BERLIN
- CAROLINA
- PASSPORT
- LONDON

Names for Musical Horses

- MOZART
- JACKSON
- BEETHOVEN
- DANCER
- DICKINSON
- MADONNA
- DA VINCI
- SULLIVAN
- CHOPIN

Names for Horse Pairs

If you have two horses that you must name, what a wonderful opportunity. Here are some names for horse doubles that would go great together.

- ADAM & EVE
- AFRICA & ZULU
- BAMBI & THUMPER
- MOLLY & POLLY
- RUTH & NAOMI
- SALT & PEPPER
- MICHAEL & JACKSON
- BEN & JERRY
- BATMAN & ROBIN

- FRED & BARNEY
- DAVID & GOLIATH
- WINSTON & CHURCHILL
- GARFIELD & ODIE
- MARY & RHODA
- BONNIE & CLYDE
- FLORENCE & NIGHTINGALE
- ANNE & FRANK

Don't Mind the Horse!

A horse's mind or mentality is based on behaviours that have been learnt over thousands of years. Just as we learn as we get older, so horse breeds have learnt as their families have got older. This needed to happen so that they could avoid dangers that they may have faced in the wild. As I am sure you know horses have very acute senses and particular ways of communicating with other horses. Here are some excellent things to know about how horses' function through their senses.

Senses

Horses have very special senses. They are extremely "fine-tuned". This affects the way that they are and now the behave in their surroundings.

Sight

Unlike human beings' horses have two eyes that are placed on the side of their heads, not at the front. This allows them to have what is called a "wide field of vision". This means that they can see across a wider area than humans. In addition to this they can see almost all the way behind them as well. This comes in handy for when they are in the wild as they are able to keep an eye out for predators.

Touch

Like humans, some parts of the horse's body are very sensitive to touch. They will be more confident with a person they have not seen before by touching them with their muzzle.

Smell

A horse's sense of smell helps them to find out if there are predictors on the loose. Some smells that they are not used to make them nervous

Taste

Just like their sense of smell horses have sensitive palates. Unlike humans, they do not play with their food... if they don't like it, they will reject it and walk away quite quickly!

Breed Under the Microscope

BREED: AKHAL TEKE

Warmblood

Origin: Turkoman Steppes

Height: 15HH

Colour: Black, Chestnut, Grey or Bay in most cases with a metallic sheen

Physique: long head, elegant, straight profile, thin neck and lengthy legs,

Temperament: stubborn and forthright

Jobs: Used for riding

The Akhal-Teke is a beautiful horse from Turkmenistan. They are known for their speed and ability to keep going for a long time. It is thought that they are one of the oldest ever horse breeds.

Horse Colours

Bay

Black

Grey

Brown

Blue Dun

Yellow Dun

Palomino

Spotted

Strawberry Roan

Bay-Brown

Black-Brown

Cream or Cremello

Liver Chestnut

Chestnut

Roan

Piebald

Skewbald

Pinto

Albino

Odd-coloured

Whole Coloured

The hairs the cover a horse's skin are at a special angle as they give the horse protection again the elements. Rain, wind and everything like that. There are many different lengths and colours of hair dependant on the breed of the horse.

Describing a Horse

There are different ways that provide us with the key information of the height, age and sex of a horse. If you were blessed and had someone buy you a horse, there would be several things to consider. There are two important parts that need to be considered when looking at a horse. Its physical shape and its character.

So... let's look at one of the basics

What is a horse?

The word horse is a general term used to describe both horses and ponies of both sexes. The species of animal that horses belong to is called Equidae

What is the difference between a horse and a pony?

Horses are known as equines. Like you have a last name "Equine" is their last name. The main **difference between ponies** and **horses** is their height. **A horse** is usually considered to be an equine that's at least 14.2 hands tall. **A pony** is an equine less than 14.2 hands.

There are also some other differences. Ponies can be a lot wider than horses, have shorter noses and wider faces.

Are Unicorns Real?

Here is the big question! Researcher's from Russia found a unicorn skull in Russia. This is amazing news! However, girls the bad news is that the unicorn didn't look like how we imagine them to look. They were more like Rhinos. Some scientists described them as being about 6 feet tall and around 9,000 pounds. This means that they were really tall and really heavy! But they didn't look like a horse. They looked more like a woolly mammoth with a big horn coming out the top of its head!

A really cool fact is that these unicorns are thought to have lasted a lot longer than the other prehistoric animals. People think that it was due to their migration patterns throughout the year.

So, in answer to the big question! Yes! Unicorns did exist!

Put Your Shoes on!

If a horse is to walk on a tarmacked road it is important that its feet are protected by metal shoes. The reason horses wear shoes on their hooves it to protect the walls of the hoof and stop it for wearing away.

Hooves are like finger nails and so they are always growing. Just like your nails need to be trimmed, horses' hooves must be trimmed or they can become lame. A horse should have his shoes renewed every 4-6 weeks by a farrier or a blacksmith.

Types of Shoes

Just like we have different shoes, such as school shoes, trainers and wellington boots, so do horses!

Below is a long list of shoes.

Feather-edged shoe

Used for horses that hit their opposite leg when the walk. They are made so that there is little chance of the Horse hurting itself.

Plain stamped shoe

This is the simplest shoe. It is made by having a straight bar of iron that is shaped and stamped. These shoes are very good wearing and most horses wear them.

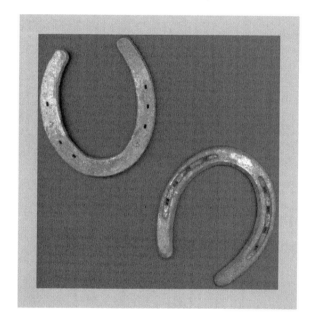

The Hunter Shoe

This shoe is used by horses that work on grass. This is especially good for horses that have to stop quickly as it prevents them from slipping.

Surgical Shoe

This shoe is for horses with problems such as corns and laminitis.

Racing Plate

This is a light weight shoe that is made of aluminium. It is made for racing horses and show pony's and is really good for surfaces such as grass and sand

Breed Under the Microscope

BREED: SHIRE

Coldblood

Origin: United Kingdom and Central based countries

Height: Approximately 17HH

Colour: Dark with White Markings

Physique: Broad Forehead, Crested neck, broad back and silky skin. Strong and one of the tallest breeds in the world

Jobs: Can be used for show, agricultural work and riding

Be Stable!

One of the places that a horse can be kept is a stable. The stables need to be kept warm and dry for the horse. To do this it needs to be full of clean bedding, straw and hay. This needs to be changed often so that the horse can lay down if needs be.

Different Types of Bedding

I am sure that you have different bedding that you put on your bed, and it's the same for horses. Here are a few options for horses.

Straw

Oat Straw: Tastes really nice so the horses may actually eat it

Barley Straw: Can be quite rough so it may irritate the horse's skin when the lay down.

Wheat Straw: Known as the best straw for horses bedding because it is very light, not dusty and drains very well.

Wood Shavings

Wood shavings are clean and can be eat. They are lovely and warm and comfortable for any horse.

Shredded Paper

This type of bedding is very warm and is also free of dust. One of the negatives however is that when it's wet it can become very heavy. Also, if there is ink on the paper, this isn't good for the horses

Peat Moss

This bedding is known to keep the horses very warm and very comfortable, however, it is quite expensive. It is also difficult to maintain as it must be laid thickly in the stable and needs to be cleared out and raked often.

Grooming a Horse

It is important that stabled horses are groomed every day, normally for about 1 hour. The reason they are groomed is to keep their skin healthy, keep their coats shiny and massage their muscles.

If you have been around horses you will have noticed that if they are together, many times they will groom each other. It is almost like a way that you would look after a friend.

You may have also seen them roll on their backs. This is done because horses do not have fingers like we do to scratch our backs if we have an itch. They use the ground to do this for them!

Grooming tools

Body Brush

Dandy Brush

Curry Comb

Mane and tail comb

Water Brush

Hoof pick

Hoof Oil

Horses Behaving Badly!

In most cases horses that are trained well don't really behave badly. If they do, just like us, it must be for a reason. Some horses act badly initially but can be trained to be better behaved. Just like us!

Fear is normally the biggest cause of bad behaviour in horses. When a horse is scared or unsure of what to do it will misbehave. Also, in many cases it can come from a horse trying to defend itself.

An example of this is if a horse is being handled badly by its rider. If this happens then the horse may kick or barge or bite. Also, if a horse is bored or frustrated it will normally play up a little bit.

Nevertheless, here are some of the traits of bad behaved horses.

Rough Handling

This can lead to biting barging and sometimes barging. Other horses have quite aggressive natures, so their handlers must be strong.

Napping

This is a special name for a horse that decides that it doesn't want to do what the rider says under any circumstance. They will do things like stopping dead in it tracks or completely turn around and run back to its stable.

Rearing

This is when a horse stands up on its hind legs. If a horse keeps doing this, it's important that the owner finds out if the horse is in pain. This can actually happen accidently if the rider is asking him to move forward but then pulls back on the reins.

If you are on a horse and it rears up when you are on it, sit forward and do not pull on the reins.

Biting

Sometimes biting horses will make their ears go flat and look to nibble anyone who handles him. Biting is a very bad habit for a horse to have. If you have a horse that bites don't let them get away with it, tell them NO very firmly.

Rolling

Rolling is quite natural for all members of the horse family. It is quite healthy. Nevertheless, a horse that continuously rolls could actually have tummy ache meaning that a vet should be called.

Kicking

This can be a serious habit that like biting must be stopped as soon as it begins. Some horses can kick just because of being sensitive when being groomed. Make sure you are carful by never standing behind a horse. Being kicked by a horse is a very painful thing. ⎯

How to Ride

Before you actually ride a horse, you must learn how to get onto it. Make sure that you check and tighten the "girth" so that the saddle doesn't slip whilst you are on the horse.

1.Firstly, face the saddle and move the leathers so that the stirrup iron reaches to the top of your arm.

2. Stand in front of the horse to make sure everything is level.

3. Stand with your left shoulder to the horses left shoulder

4. Hold the reins in your left hand and put your left hand in front of the horse's withers.

5.Hold the stirrup with your right hand and put your left foot into the stirrup iron.

6.Face the horse and take the waist of the saddle with your right hand and pull yourself up onto the horse.

7.Swing your right leg up and over the back of the horse

8.Sit on the saddle

9. Put your right foot in the right stirrup iron and hold the reins in both hands.

Breed Under the Microscope

BREED: CLEAVELAND BAY HORSE

Warmblood

Origin: Yorkshire, England

Height: 16HH

Colour: Bay or Brown

Physique: Large Head, Long back, High Tail, Excellent Profile

Temperament: Calm, Clever and Sensible

Jobs: Riding and Driving

Horse Activities for You to Get Involved in!

Dressage

This consists of movements that the horse and rider perform to show that they are together as one team. One team in harmony. It is now very popular as a sport, however, historically it was used as an exercise in the olden days to train cavalry horses.

Show Jumping

These competitions can take place outdoor or indoor. They generally have two rounds. The aim of the first round it to complete the course without knocking down any jumps.

Those who complete the first round do something called a jump off to decide who wins the championship.

Horse Trials

These trials are often called "Events". They can be run between 1-3 days. On many three-day events horses and riders are asked to complete both Dressage and Show jumping events. It is like a triathlon for horses.

As you can see, there are so many ways you can get involved in activities with horses.

How to muck out!

If a horse's home is in a stable, it's important that everything is comfortable for him. His bedding needs to be changed regularly...just like yours!

His stables must be cleaned out at least once a day!

Every morning the horse's droppings should be taken away. The floor should be swept and then the bedding raked and levelled.

Breed Under the Microscope

BREED: CRIOLLO

Warmblood

Origin: Argentina

Height: 14.2HH

Colour: Dun with dark points, dorsal stripe with dark parts. red and blue roan, sorrel and skewbald

Physique: Short coupled, sturdy frame, short head, sloping shoulders, short legs and hard feet.

Temperament: Very willing, very reliable, very strong

Jobs: Long treks and work

Best Horse Books!

For this section it's best if I hand over to Gracie. She loves horse books! Over to you Gracie!

Hi Everyone. I like you, love horse books. I read them all the time. Underneath is a list of my most favourite horse books of all time? Have you read any of these? Which is your favourite?

Black Beauty

A Horse of Kate

War Horse

The Horse and his Boy

Blue Ribbon Trail Ride

The Runaway Pony

High Hurdles Series

Schleich Horses

If you love horses, you will love Schleich models. Gracie's room is completely full of them.

Schleich is one of the world's leading toy manufacturers and is based in Germany. They love children to use their imaginations.

Careers for Horse Mad Girls

There are many different career options for girls who are totally and utterly obsessed with horses. Here are some career possibilities that you may be interested in working towards. They range from veterinarian to horse breeder. Which ones do you like?

1. Equine Veterinarian

Equine veterinarians provide preventive health care for horses and treat them if they are hurt. Becoming a licensed equine veterinarian means you will have to work very hard at school; doing well in the sciences including biology. It is likely that you would then be able to study this at university!

2. Mounted Police Officer

Mounted police officers use their horses to protect big crowds at big events. You may have seen them before. Mounted officers must first train to become normal police officers. Then they are able to transfer and become special mounted officers.

3. Equine Veterinary Technician

Equine veterinary technicians help vets as they complete exams and surgical procedures. Vet techs must complete a two-year university degree and pass an exam to become licensed in the field.

4. Riding Instructor

Riding instructors help students and direct them in riding lessons and training sessions. Instructors may specialize in a lot of different of riding disciplines such as dressage and show jumping.

5. Broodmare Manager

Broodmare managers work in the care of mares and foals. They are responsible for assisting with foaling, teasing mares, and keeping detailed records. They are like a midwife for horses!

6. Farrier

Farriers are responsible for trimming, maintaining, and balancing equine hooves. Farriers must visit each client about 5 times per year on average. Many farriers are self-employed and can learn the trade via an apprenticeship course.

7. Jockey

A jockey rides racehorses in flat or fenced races according to the trainer's instructions. Jockeys can ride many races each day, as well as working with horses in the morning.

8. Exercise Rider

Exercise riders ride horses every morning on the racetrack, following the instructions they're given by trainers.

9. Groom

Grooms provide daily care for the horses. In many cases they know the horse the best and so take care to notice any changes in a horse's behaviour or body that might signal a need for veterinary care.

10. Horse Breeder

Horse breeders arrange for specific horses, with specific qualities to some together so that foals of a certain breed or foals that are suited for a specific type of competition are made!

11. Barn Manager

Barn managers supervise the care of the horses in their stable.

12. Racehorse Trainer

Racehorse trainers work with their horse to help them compete in races. They will know all the big races that are coming up, the ground that the horse will be running on and the best way to prepare the horse to try and win.

13. Equine Dental Technician

Equine dental technicians are dentists for horses! Good dental care ensures that the horse can eat and perform properly.

Which job do you think would interest you!

Important Horse Terms to Know!

Ancestor

A member of the family that lived a long time ago

Bit

The part of the bridle that goes into the horse's mouth

Blacksmith

A Blacksmith is someone who makes things with iron. Sometimes this can be horse shoes.

Breeding Stock

A mare or stallion that is intended for breeding work. They are normally chosen because of their good qualities.

Bridle

A piece of horse headgear made up of leather straps

Curry Comb	A square or rectangular or oval comb with rubber or plastic teeth used for grooming horses
Dam	A Mother Horse
Dandy Brush	A brush with harsh wiry bristles used for grooming horses.
Domesticated	An animal that is used to living alongside humans
Farrier	A farrier is a blacksmith that does horseshoeing but doesn't necessarily do other work with iron.
Gelding	A male horse that has had an operation to stop it producing offspring

Hogging	A Horse mane that has been completely shaved
Holter	Horse headgear that is sometimes made of rope.
Listless	Lifeless; not wanting to do anything
Mare	An Adult female horse
Muzzle	The sticking out part of an animal's face that includes their nose and mouth.
Stallion	An Adult horse that can produce offspring
Roughage	Fibre from grasses and other long-stemmed plants
Steeplechase	A horse race over an obstacle course or open country

Taut	Stretched or Tightened
Turnout	The time when the horse is out of the confinement of the stable and loose in a larger area.
Withers	The top of a horse's shoulder blade

Journal

Printed in Great Britain
by Amazon

36625325R00070